Double Trouble!

Pregnancy Journal When You're Expecting Twins

Copyright 2016

Twin
BABY

Month 1

how do i feel? _______________________

____

____

____

- ☐ higher ♥ rate?
- ☐ emotional?
- ☐ warmer hands&feet?
- ☐ acne?
- ☐ increased thirst
- ☐ veins more noticeable in breast?

Waist Measurement : _____________

Weight : ____________

Milestone : ____________

____

____

____

____

____

photo
here

Twin
BABY

With
LOVE

photo
here

Twin
BABY

With
LOVE

photo
here

Twin
BABY

photo
here

Month 2

how do i feel? ________________________

____

____

____

- [ ] higher ♥ rate?
- [ ] emotional?
- [ ] warmer hands&feet?
- [ ] acne?
- [ ] increased thirst
- [ ] veins more noticeable in breast?

Twins

Waist Measurement : __________

Weight : __________

Milestone : __________

____

____

____

____

____

cravings :

preparations for the twins

photo
here

Twin
BABY

With
LOVE

photo
here

Twin
BABY

photo
here

Twin
BABY

With
LOVE

photo
here

Month 3

how do i feel?________________________

____

____

____

☐ higher ♥ rate?   ☐ acne?

☐ emotional?   ☐ increased thirst

☐ warmer hands&feet?   ☐ veins more noticeable in breast?

Waist Measurement : __________

Weight : __________

Milestone : __________

____

____

____

____

____

cravings :

Twins

preparations for the twins

photo
here

Twin
BABY

photo
here

Twin
BABY

photo
here

Twin
BABY

photo
here

Month 4

how do i feel? _______________________

____

____

____

- ☐ higher ♥ rate?
- ☐ emotional?
- ☐ warmer hands&feet?

- ☐ acne?
- ☐ increased thirst
- ☐ veins more noticeable in breast?

Twins

Waist Measurement : __________

Weight : __________

Milestone : __________

____

____

____

____

____

cravings :

preparations for the twins

photo
here

Twin
BABY

With
LOVE

photo
here

Twin
BABY

With
LOVE

photo
here

Twin
BABY

photo
here

Month 5

how do i feel? _______________________

____

____

____

Twins

☐ higher ♥ rate?　　☐ acne?

☐ emotional?　　　　☐ increased thirst

☐ warmer hands&feet?　☐ veins more noticeable in breast?

Waist Measurement : __________

Weight : __________

Milestone : __________

____

____

____

____

____

cravings :

preparations
for the twins

With
LOVE

photo
here

Twin
BABY

With
LOVE

photo
here

Twin
BABY

photo
here

Twin
BABY

With
LOVE

photo
here

Month 6

how do i feel? _______________________

____

____

____

Twins

☐ higher ♥ rate? ☐ acne?

☐ emotional? ☐ increased thirst

☐ warmer hands&feet? ☐ veins more noticeable in breast?

Waist Measurement : _________

Weight : _________

Milestone : _________

____

____

____

____

____

cravings :

preparations for the twins

With
LOVE

photo
here

Twin
BABY

photo
here

Twin
BABY

photo
here

Twin
BABY

photo
here
With
LOVE

Month 7

how do i feel? _______________________

____

____

____

☐ higher ♥ rate?   ☐ acne?

☐ emotional?   ☐ increased thirst

☐ warmer hands&feet?   ☐ veins more noticeable in breast?

Waist Measurement : ___________

Weight : ___________

Milestone : ___________

____

____

____

____

____

photo
here

Twin
BABY

With
LOVE

photo
here

Twin
BABY

With
LOVE

photo
here

Twin
BABY

With
LOVE

photo
here

Month 8

how do i feel? ______________________________

____

____

____

☐ higher ♥ rate?　　　　☐ acne?

☐ emotional?　　　　　　☐ increased thirst

☐ warmer hands&feet?　　☐ veins more noticeable in breast?

Twins

Waist Measurement : __________

Weight : __________

Milestone : __________

____

____

____

____

____

cravings :

photo
here

Twin
BABY

With
LOVE

photo
here

Twin
BABY

photo
here

Twin
BABY

photo
here

Month 9

how do i feel? _______________________

____

____

____

- ☐ higher ♥ rate?
- ☐ emotional?
- ☐ warmer hands&feet?
- ☐ acne?
- ☐ increased thirst
- ☐ veins more noticeable in breast?

Waist Measurement : _______________

Weight : _______________

Milestone : _______________

____

____

____

____

____

With
LOVE

photo
here

Twin
BABY

With
LOVE

photo
here

Twin
BABY

With
LOVE

photo
here

Twin
BABY

With
LOVE

photo
here